EXPLORE THE WORLD

SOCIAL SCIENCE

S0-CYD-622

Monkey Trouble

MAUREEN ASH

TABLE OF CONTENTS

PIONEER VALLEY EDUCATIONAL PRESS, INC

A CITY FULL OF MONKEYS

It's fun to visit the monkeys at the zoo. We like to watch them play and climb and chatter. Sometimes, when they sit and look at us or care for their babies, we laugh at how cute they are. Sometimes we talk about how much they seem like us.

But in some parts of the world, monkeys live in cities right alongside people. They gather near the roads. They play in the fountains. They swing up in the trees above streets and houses. It may sound fun to have monkeys all around you but, in some places, it is not fun at all.

In New Delhi, India, thousands of small rhesus (*REE-sis*) monkeys live in the city. They steal food from street **vendors**. They sneak into people's houses and leave a mess. They climb up and damage power lines, knocking out electricity. Sometimes they threaten and even bite people.

It's a big problem! Lots of people would like to just get rid of the monkeys.

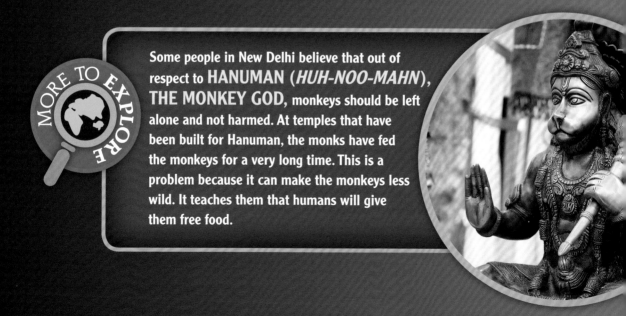

MORE TO EXPLORE

Some people in New Delhi believe that out of respect to **HANUMAN** (*HUH-NOO-MAHN*), **THE MONKEY GOD,** monkeys should be left alone and not harmed. At temples that have been built for Hanuman, the monks have fed the monkeys for a very long time. This is a problem because it can make the monkeys less wild. It teaches them that humans will give them free food.

CHINA

PAKISTAN

NEW DELHI

NEPAL

BHUTAN

BANGLADESH

INDIA

SRI
LANKA

5

So why is it such a big problem lately? New Delhi used to have forests around it where the monkeys lived in the wild. But more and more people are moving to the city. Every year the city grows, and more of the forest is cut down.

In fact, most of the monkeys are not moving into the city; the city is moving out to the monkeys. Monkeys are smart animals who can adjust to new **conditions**. They can be a lot like people. And now monkeys are learning to live in the city.

MONKEY, GO!

At one time, the city paid people to catch the monkeys in cages and take them to forest areas outside the city.

People would drive trucks with fruit and other food to the monkeys to keep them from returning to the city to look for stuff to eat. This seemed like a good idea, but forests were not large enough anymore for all the monkeys. Also, it was difficult for the monkey catchers to capture all of the monkeys.

Another reason this did not work well is that the monkeys live in family groups, just like people. The monkey catchers would capture monkeys, but they did not know which ones were in which family. Monkey families that are split up become even more **aggressive** toward people, which added to the trouble they already caused.

A group of rhesus monkeys is called a troop.

Some business owners solve the monkey problem with more monkeys! Rhesus monkeys are small, about the size of a house cat. They are afraid of langur monkeys, which are larger.

A few monkey trainers have trained langurs to chase away the smaller monkeys. They go around to hotels or other businesses on bikes or motorcycles with langur monkeys sitting behind them. The langur monkey hops off the bike and scares the rhesus monkeys away.

Once the place is clear of rhesus monkeys, the langur monkey comes back to the bike. The owner gets paid, and they move on to the next job.

But that only solves the problem for a short time because the rhesus monkeys always come back. And it makes things worse for the neighbors who have to put up with the extra monkeys that are **fleeing** the langurs.

rhesus monkey

langur
monkey

WHOSE HOME?

Monkeys are a problem in many cities throughout India and across the rest of Asia.

In some places in Japan, snow monkeys break into people's homes. They steal food and sometimes trash houses. They also get into crops that farmers are growing and eat the fruit and vegetables. They can do a lot of damage.

These snow monkeys have not lost their homes to a city. Instead, the forests where the monkeys lived were cut down and replaced by tree farms. The farms do not have as many kinds of plants as a real forest. There is nothing there for the monkeys to eat. The snow monkeys are just trying to find a way to survive. They need food to eat. That brings them into contact with humans. This can be uncomfortable for the humans and the monkeys.

The problem of monkeys living too close to humans will not be solved easily. Most people like monkeys and do not want to hurt them, but they do not want monkeys in their homes either.

There is a good chance that the monkeys feel the same way about us.

Where in the World

Do Rhesus Monkeys Live?

Stripes on map show places where rhesus monkeys live today

AFGHANISTAN

PAKISTAN

NEPAL

BHUTAN

SOUTHERN CHINA

INDIA

BANGLADESH

VIETNAM

LAOS

MYANMAR (BURMA)

THAILAND

How can the monkey problem be solved?
No one is sure. But if we do not find some way
to **preserve** the homes of wild creatures,
they may end up in ours!

GLOSSARY

aggressive
ready and willing to fight

conditions
ways of living or existing

fleeing
running away from danger

preserve
to keep (something) safe from
harm or loss

vendors
people who sell things, especially
on the street

INDEX